paperblanks®
DAYPLANNERS

paperblanks®

DIARY

2016

paperblanks®
DIARIES

NAME _____

PHONE _____

IN CASE OF EMERGENCY, PLEASE CONTACT

NAME _____

PHONE _____

2016

JANUARY
M	T	W	T	F	S	S
28	29	30	31	1	2	**3**
4	5	6	7	8	9	**10**
11	12	13	14	15	16	**17**
18	19	20	21	22	23	**24**
25	26	27	28	29	30	**31**

FEBRUARY
M	T	W	T	F	S	S
1	2	3	4	5	6	**7**
8	9	10	11	12	13	**14**
15	16	17	18	19	20	**21**
22	23	24	25	26	27	**28**
29	1	2	3	4	5	6

MARCH
M	T	W	T	F	S	S
29	1	2	3	4	5	**6**
7	8	9	10	11	12	**13**
14	15	16	17	18	19	**20**
21	22	23	24	25	26	**27**
28	29	30	31	1	2	3

APRIL
M	T	W	T	F	S	S
28	29	30	31	1	2	**3**
4	5	6	7	8	9	**10**
11	12	13	14	15	16	**17**
18	19	20	21	22	23	**24**
25	26	27	28	29	30	1

MAY
M	T	W	T	F	S	S
25	26	27	28	29	30	**1**
2	3	4	5	6	7	**8**
9	10	11	12	13	14	**15**
16	17	18	19	20	21	**22**
$^{23}/_{30}$ $^{24}/_{31}$	25	26	27	28	29	

JUNE
M	T	W	T	F	S	S
30	31	1	2	3	4	**5**
6	7	8	9	10	11	**12**
13	14	15	16	17	18	**19**
20	21	22	23	24	25	**26**
27	28	29	30	1	2	3

JULY
M	T	W	T	F	S	S
27	28	29	30	1	2	**3**
4	5	6	7	8	9	**10**
11	12	13	14	15	16	**17**
18	19	20	21	22	23	**24**
25	26	27	28	29	30	**31**

AUGUST
M	T	W	T	F	S	S
1	2	3	4	5	6	**7**
8	9	10	11	12	13	**14**
15	16	17	18	19	20	**21**
22	23	24	25	26	27	**28**
29	30	31	1	2	3	4

SEPTEMBER
M	T	W	T	F	S	S
29	30	31	1	2	3	**4**
5	6	7	8	9	10	**11**
12	13	14	15	16	17	**18**
19	20	21	22	23	24	**25**
26	27	28	29	30	1	2

OCTOBER
M	T	W	T	F	S	S
26	27	28	29	30	1	**2**
3	4	5	6	7	8	**9**
10	11	12	13	14	15	**16**
17	18	19	20	21	22	**23**
$^{24}/_{31}$	25	26	27	28	29	**30**

NOVEMBER
M	T	W	T	F	S	S
31	1	2	3	4	5	**6**
7	8	9	10	11	12	**13**
14	15	16	17	18	19	**20**
21	22	23	24	25	26	**27**
28	29	30	1	2	3	4

DECEMBER
M	T	W	T	F	S	S
28	29	30	1	2	3	**4**
5	6	7	8	9	10	**11**
12	13	14	15	16	17	**18**
19	20	21	22	23	24	**25**
26	27	28	29	30	31	1

LEGEND FOR SYMBOLS

Moon Phases

☽ FIRST QUARTER

☾ LAST QUARTER

○ FULL MOON

● NEW MOON

❋ FIRST DAY OF SPRING

🍂 FIRST DAY OF AUTUMN

✹ SHORTEST DAY

☼ LONGEST DAY

🕒 DAYLIGHT SAVING TIME BEGINS/ENDS

HOLIDAYS & CELEBRATIONS 2016

JANUARY
Friday 1 New Year's Day
Saturday 2 Second of January (Scot.)

FEBRUARY
Monday 8 Chinese New Year
Tuesday 9 Shrove Tuesday
Pancake Day
Wednesday 10 Ash Wednesday
Sunday 14 Valentine's Day

MARCH
Tuesday 1 St David's Day
Saturday 5 St Piran's Day
Sunday 6 Mother's Day
Thursday 17 St Patrick's Day (IE, NI)
Sunday 20 Palm Sunday
Thursday 24 Purim*
Friday 25 Good Friday (UK)
Sunday 27 Easter
Monday 28 Easter Monday
(except Scot.)

APRIL
Friday 1 April Fools' Day
Saturday 23 Passover*
St George's Day

MAY
Sunday 1 May Day
Monday 2 Bank Holiday
Sunday 15 Whitsun
Monday 30 Bank Holiday (UK)

JUNE
Monday 6 Ramadan begins
Bank Holiday (IE)

Sunday 12 Shavuot
Sunday 19 Father's Day

JULY
Wednesday 6 Eid al-Fitr*
Tuesday 12 Battle of the Boyne (NI)
Friday 15 St Swithin's Day

AUGUST
Monday 1 Bank Holiday (IE, Scot.)
Monday 29 Bank Holiday
(UK except Scot.)

SEPTEMBER
Sunday 11 Eid al-Adha*

OCTOBER
Sunday 2 Muharram begins
Monday 3 Rosh Hashanah*
Wednesday 12 Yom Kippur
Monday 17 Sukkot*
Monday 31 Halloween
Bank Holiday (IE)

NOVEMBER
Saturday 5 Guy Fawkes Night
Sunday 6 Remembrance Sunday
Wednesday 30 St Andrew's Day (Scot.)

DECEMBER
Sunday 11 Mawlid al-Nabi
Sunday 25 Christmas Day
Hanukkah*
Monday 26 Boxing Day (UK)
St Stephen's Day (IE)
Saturday 31 New Year's Eve
Hogmanay (Scot.)*

Additional public holidays may precede or follow this date.

NOTES

JANUARY – 2016 MONTH PLANNER

MONDAY	TUESDAY	WEDNESDAY	THURSDAY	FRIDAY	SATURDAY	SUNDAY
28	29	30	31 New Year's Eve Hogmanay (Scot.)	1 New Year's Day	2 Second of January (Scot.)	3
4	5	6	7	8	9	10
11	12	13	14	15	16	17
18	19	20	21	22	23	24
25	26	27	28	29	30	31

FEBRUARY – 2016 MONTH PLANNER

MONDAY	TUESDAY	WEDNESDAY	THURSDAY	FRIDAY	SATURDAY	SUNDAY
1 Chinese New Year	2	3	4	5	6	7
8	9 Shrove Tuesday Pancake Day	10	11	12	13	14 Valentine's Day
15	16	17 Ash Wednesday	18	19	20	21
22	23	24	25	26	27	28
29	1 St David's Day	2	3	4	5 St Piran's Day	6 Mother's Day

MARCH – 2016 MONTH PLANNER

MONDAY	TUESDAY	WEDNESDAY	THURSDAY	FRIDAY	SATURDAY	SUNDAY
29	1	2	3	4	5	6
7	8 St David's Day	9	10	11	12 St Piran's Day	13 Mother's Day
14	15	16	17 St Patrick's Day (IE, NI)	18	19	20
21	22	23	24	25 Good Friday (UK)	26	27 Palm Sunday
28 Easter Monday (except Scot.)	29	30	31 Purim	1 April Fools' Day	2	3 Easter

APRIL – 2016 MONTH PLANNER

MONDAY	TUESDAY	WEDNESDAY	THURSDAY	FRIDAY	SATURDAY	SUNDAY
28	29	30	31	1	2	3
4 Easter Monday (except Scot.)	5	6	7	8 April Fools' Day	9	10
11	12	13	14	15	16	17
18	19	20	21	22	23	24
25	26	27	28	29	30 Passover St George's Day	1 May Day

MAY – 2016 MONTH PLANNER

MONDAY	TUESDAY	WEDNESDAY	THURSDAY	FRIDAY	SATURDAY	SUNDAY
25	26	27	28	29	30	1
2	3	4	5	6	7	May Day 8
Bank Holiday 9	10	11	12	13	14	15
16	17	18	19	20	21	Whitsun 22
23	24	25	26	27	28	29
30 Bank Holiday (UK)	31					

JUNE – 2016 MONTH PLANNER

MONDAY	TUESDAY	WEDNESDAY	THURSDAY	FRIDAY	SATURDAY	SUNDAY
30	31	1	2	3	4	5
Bank Holiday (UK) 6	7	8	9	10	11	12
Ramadan begins Bank Holiday (IE) 13	14	15	16	17	18	Shavuot 19
20	21	22	23	24	25	Father's Day 26
27	28	29	30	1	2	3

JULY – 2016 MONTH PLANNER

MONDAY	TUESDAY	WEDNESDAY	THURSDAY	FRIDAY	SATURDAY	SUNDAY
27	28	29	30	1	2	3
4	5	6	7	8	9	10
11	12	13 Eid al-Fitr	14	15	16	17
18	19 Battle of the Boyne (NI)	20	21	22 St Swithin's Day	23	24
25	26	27	28	29	30	31

AUGUST – 2016 MONTH PLANNER

MONDAY	TUESDAY	WEDNESDAY	THURSDAY	FRIDAY	SATURDAY	SUNDAY
1 Bank Holiday (IE, Scot.)	2	3	4	5	6	7
8	9	10	11	12	13	14
15	16	17	18	19	20	21
22	23	24	25	26	27	28
29 Bank Holiday (UK except Scot.)	30	31	1	2	3	4

SEPTEMBER – 2016 MONTH PLANNER

MONDAY	TUESDAY	WEDNESDAY	THURSDAY	FRIDAY	SATURDAY	SUNDAY
29	30	31	1	2	3	4
5 Bank Holiday (UK except Scot.)	6	7	8	9	10	11
12	13	14	15	16	17	18 Eid al-Adha
19	20	21	22	23	24	25
26	27	28	29	30	1	2 Muharram begins

OCTOBER – 2016 MONTH PLANNER

MONDAY	TUESDAY	WEDNESDAY	THURSDAY	FRIDAY	SATURDAY	SUNDAY
26	27	28	29	30	1	2
3	4	5	6	7	8	Muharram begins 9
Rosh Hashanah 10	11	12	13	14	15	16
17	18	Yom Kippur 19	20	21	22	23
24	25	26	27	28	29	30
Sukkot 31 Halloween Bank Holiday (IE)						

NOVEMBER – 2016 MONTH PLANNER

MONDAY	TUESDAY	WEDNESDAY	THURSDAY	FRIDAY	SATURDAY	SUNDAY
31 Halloween Bank Holiday (IE)	1	2	3	4	5	6
7	8	9	10	11	12 Guy Fawkes Night	13 Remembrance Sunday
14	15	16	17	18	19	20
21	22	23	24	25	26	27
28	29	30 St Andrew's Day (Scot.)	1	2	3	4

DECEMBER – 2016 MONTH PLANNER

MONDAY	TUESDAY	WEDNESDAY	THURSDAY	FRIDAY	SATURDAY	SUNDAY
28	29	30 St Andrew's Day (Scot.)	1	2	3	4
5	6	7	8	9	10	11
12	13	14	15	16	17	18 Mawlid al-Nabi
19	20	21 ✳	22	23	24	25 Christmas Day Hanukkah
26 Boxing Day (UK) St Stephen's Day (IE)	27	28	29	30	31 New Year's Eve Hogmanay (Scot.)	1 New Year's Day

NOTES

THE YEAR
2016

DECEMBER–JANUARY

MONDAY
28

TUESDAY
29

WEDNESDAY
30

THURSDAY
31
NEW YEAR'S EVE
HOGMANAY (SCOT.)

FRIDAY

1

NEW YEAR'S DAY

SATURDAY

2 ☾

SECOND OF JANUARY
  (SCOT.)

SUNDAY

3

NOTES

DECEMBER

	M	T	W	T	F	S	**S**
49	30	1	2	3	4	5	**6**
50	7	8	9	10	11	12	**13**
51	14	15	16	17	18	19	**20**
52	21	22	23	24	25	26	**27**
53	28	29	30	31	1	2	3

JANUARY

MONDAY
4

TUESDAY
5

WEDNESDAY
6

THURSDAY
7

FRIDAY
8

SATURDAY
9

SUNDAY
10 ●

NOTES

	M	T	W	T	F	S	S
53	28	29	30	31	1	2	**3**
1	4	5	6	7	8	9	**10**
2	11	12	13	14	15	16	**17**
3	18	19	20	21	22	23	**24**
4	25	26	27	28	29	30	**31**

JANUARY

MONDAY
11

TUESDAY
12

WEDNESDAY
13

THURSDAY
14

FRIDAY
15

SATURDAY
16 ☽

SUNDAY
17

NOTES

JANUARY

	M	T	W	T	F	S	S
53	28	29	30	31	1	2	**3**
1	4	5	6	7	8	9	**10**
2	11	12	13	14	15	16	**17**
3	18	19	20	21	22	23	**24**
4	25	26	27	28	29	30	**31**

JANUARY

MONDAY
18

TUESDAY
19

WEDNESDAY
20

THURSDAY
21

FRIDAY
22

SATURDAY
23

SUNDAY
24 ○

NOTES

JANUARY

	M	T	W	T	F	S	S
53	28	29	30	31	1	2	**3**
1	4	5	6	7	8	9	**10**
2	11	12	13	14	15	16	**17**
3	18	19	20	21	22	23	**24**
4	25	26	27	28	29	30	**31**

JANUARY

MONDAY
25

TUESDAY
26

WEDNESDAY
27

THURSDAY
28

FRIDAY
29

SATURDAY
30

SUNDAY
31

NOTES

	M	T	W	T	F	S	S
53	28	29	30	31	1	2	**3**
1	4	5	6	7	8	9	**10**
2	11	12	13	14	15	16	**17**
3	18	19	20	21	22	23	**24**
4	25	26	27	28	29	30	**31**

FEBRUARY

MONDAY
1 ☾

TUESDAY
2

WEDNESDAY
3

THURSDAY
4

2016

FRIDAY
5

SATURDAY
6

SUNDAY
7

NOTES

FEBRUARY

M	T	W	T	F	S	S
5	1	2	3	4	5	6	7
6	8	9	10	11	12	13	14
7	15	16	17	18	19	20	21
8	22	23	24	25	26	27	28
9	29	1	2	3	4	5	6

FEBRUARY

MONDAY
8 ●
CHINESE NEW YEAR

TUESDAY
9
SHROVE TUESDAY
PANCAKE DAY

WEDNESDAY
10
ASH WEDNESDAY

THURSDAY
11

2016

FRIDAY
12

SATURDAY
13

SUNDAY
14
VALENTINE'S DAY

NOTES

FEBRUARY

	M	T	W	T	F	S	**S**
5	1	2	3	4	5	6	**7**
6	8	9	10	11	12	13	**14**
7	15	16	17	18	19	20	**21**
8	22	23	24	25	26	27	**28**
9	29	1	2	3	4	5	6

FEBRUARY

MONDAY
15 ☽

TUESDAY
16

WEDNESDAY
17

THURSDAY
18

FRIDAY
19

SATURDAY
20

SUNDAY
21

NOTES

FEBRUARY

M	T	W	T	F	S	S
5	1	2	3	4	5	6	7
6	8	9	10	11	12	13	14
7	15	16	17	18	19	20	21
8	22	23	24	25	26	27	28
9	29	1	2	3	4	5	6

FEBRUARY

TUESDAY
23

WEDNESDAY
24

THURSDAY
25

FRIDAY
26

SATURDAY
27

SUNDAY
28

NOTES

FEBRUARY

M	T	W	T	F	S	S
5	1	2	3	4	5	6	**7**
6	8	9	10	11	12	13	**14**
7	15	16	17	18	19	20	**21**
8	22	23	24	25	26	27	**28**
9	29	1	2	3	4	5	6

FEBRUARY–MARCH

MONDAY
29

TUESDAY
1 ☾
ST DAVID'S DAY

WEDNESDAY
2

THURSDAY
3

FRIDAY

4

SATURDAY

5

ST PIRAN'S DAY

SUNDAY

6

MOTHER'S DAY

NOTES

MARCH

	M	T	W	T	F	S	S
9	29	1	2	3	4	5	**6**
10	7	8	9	10	11	12	**13**
11	14	15	16	17	18	19	**20**
12	21	22	23	24	25	26	**27**
13	28	29	30	31	1	2	3

MARCH

MONDAY
7

TUESDAY
8

WEDNESDAY
9

THURSDAY
10

FRIDAY
11

SATURDAY
12

SUNDAY
13

NOTES

MARCH

	M	T	W	T	F	S	S
9	29	1	2	3	4	5	**6**
10	7	8	9	10	11	12	**13**
11	14	15	16	17	18	19	**20**
12	21	22	23	24	25	26	**27**
13	28	29	30	31	1	2	3

MARCH

MONDAY
14

TUESDAY
15 ☽

WEDNESDAY
16

THURSDAY
17
ST PATRICK'S DAY (IE, NI)

2016

FRIDAY
18

SATURDAY
19

SUNDAY
20 ❀
04:30 UTC
PALM SUNDAY

NOTES

MARCH

	M	T	W	T	F	S	S
9	29	1	2	3	4	5	**6**
10	7	8	9	10	11	12	**13**
11	14	15	16	17	18	19	**20**
12	21	22	23	24	25	26	**27**
13	28	29	30	31	1	2	3

MARCH

MONDAY
21

TUESDAY
22

WEDNESDAY
23 ○

THURSDAY
24
PURIM

2016

FRIDAY
25
GOOD FRIDAY (UK)

SATURDAY
26

SUNDAY
27 ◔
EASTER

Moving rooms-

NOTES

	M	T	W	T	F	S	**S**
MARCH							
9	29	1	2	3	4	5	**6**
10	7	8	9	10	11	12	**13**
11	14	15	16	17	18	19	**20**
12	21	22	23	24	25	26	**27**
13	28	29	30	31	1	2	3

MARCH–APRIL

MONDAY
28
EASTER MONDAY
  (EXCEPT SCOT.)

TUESDAY
29

WEDNESDAY
30

THURSDAY
31 ☾

FRIDAY

1

APRIL FOOLS' DAY

SATURDAY

2

SUNDAY

3

NOTES

MARCH

	M	T	W	T	F	S	S
9	29	1	2	3	4	5	**6**
10	7	8	9	10	11	12	**13**
11	14	15	16	17	18	19	**20**
12	21	22	23	24	25	26	**27**
13	28	29	30	31	1	2	3

APRIL

MONDAY
4

TUESDAY
5

WEDNESDAY
6

THURSDAY
7 ●

2016

FRIDAY
8

SATURDAY
9

SUNDAY
10

NOTES

	M	T	W	T	F	S	S
13	28	29	30	31	1	2	**3**
14	4	5	6	7	8	9	**10**
15	11	12	13	14	15	16	**17**
16	18	19	20	21	22	23	**24**
17	25	26	27	28	29	30	1

APRIL

MONDAY
11

TUESDAY
12

WEDNESDAY
13

THURSDAY
14 ☽

FRIDAY
15

SATURDAY
16

SUNDAY
17

NOTES

APRIL

	M	T	W	T	F	S	**S**
13	28	29	30	31	1	2	**3**
14	4	5	6	7	8	9	**10**
15	11	12	13	14	15	16	**17**
16	18	19	20	21	22	23	**24**
17	25	26	27	28	29	30	1

MONDAY
18

TUESDAY
19

WEDNESDAY
20

THURSDAY
21

FRIDAY
22 ○

SATURDAY
23
PASSOVER
ST GEORGE'S DAY

SUNDAY
24

NOTES

APRIL

	M	T	W	T	F	S	**S**
13	28	29	30	31	1	2	**3**
14	4	5	6	7	8	9	**10**
15	11	12	13	14	15	16	**17**
16	18	19	20	21	22	23	**24**
17	25	26	27	28	29	30	1

APRIL–MAY

MONDAY
25

TUESDAY
26

WEDNESDAY
27

THURSDAY
28

FRIDAY
29

SATURDAY
30 ☾

SUNDAY
1
MAY DAY

NOTES

APRIL

	M	T	W	T	F	S	S
13	28	29	30	31	1	2	**3**
14	4	5	6	7	8	9	**10**
15	11	12	13	14	15	16	**17**
16	18	19	20	21	22	23	**24**
17	25	26	27	28	29	30	1

MAY

MONDAY
2
BANK HOLIDAY

TUESDAY
3

WEDNESDAY
4

THURSDAY
5

FRIDAY
6 ●

SATURDAY
7

SUNDAY
8

NOTES

MAY

	M	T	W	T	F	S	S
17	25	26	27	28	29	30	**1**
18	2	3	4	5	6	7	**8**
19	9	10	11	12	13	14	**15**
20	16	17	18	19	20	21	**22**
21	23/30	24/31	25	26	27	28	**29**

MAY

MONDAY
9

TUESDAY
10

WEDNESDAY
11

THURSDAY
12

FRIDAY
13 ☽

SATURDAY
14

SUNDAY
15
WHITSUN

NOTES

MAY

	M	T	W	T	F	S	S
17	25	26	27	28	29	30	**1**
18	2	3	4	5	6	7	**8**
19	9	10	11	12	13	14	**15**
20	16	17	18	19	20	21	**22**
21	23/30 24/31	25	26	27	28	**29**

MAY

MONDAY
16

TUESDAY
17

WEDNESDAY
18

THURSDAY
19

FRIDAY
20

SATURDAY
21 ○

SUNDAY
22

NOTES

.

MAY

	M	T	W	T	F	S	**S**
17	25	26	27	28	29	30	**1**
18	2	3	4	5	6	7	**8**
19	9	10	11	12	13	14	**15**
20	16	17	18	19	20	21	**22**
21	23/30 24/31	25	26	27	28	**29**	

MAY

MONDAY
23

TUESDAY
24

WEDNESDAY
25

THURSDAY
26

FRIDAY
27

SATURDAY
28

SUNDAY
29 ☾

NOTES

MAY						
M	T	W	T	F	S	S
17	25	26	27	28	29	30	**1**
18	2	3	4	5	6	7	**8**
19	9	10	11	12	13	14	**15**
20	16	17	18	19	20	21	**22**
21	23/30 24/31	25	26	27	28	**29**

MAY–JUNE

MONDAY
30
BANK HOLIDAY (UK)

TUESDAY
31

WEDNESDAY
1

THURSDAY
2

FRIDAY
3

SATURDAY
4

SUNDAY
5 ●

NOTES

JUNE

	M	T	W	T	F	S	S
22	30	31	1	2	3	4	**5**
23	6	7	8	9	10	11	**12**
24	13	14	15	16	17	18	**19**
25	20	21	22	23	24	25	**26**
26	27	28	29	30	1	2	3

JUNE

MONDAY
6
RAMADAN BEGINS
BANK HOLIDAY (IE)

TUESDAY
7

WEDNESDAY
8

THURSDAY
9

FRIDAY
10

SATURDAY
11

SUNDAY
12 ☽
SHAVUOT

NOTES

JUNE

	M	T	W	T	F	S	S
22	30	31	1	2	3	4	**5**
23	**6**	**7**	**8**	**9**	**10**	**11**	**12**
24	13	14	15	16	17	18	**19**
25	20	21	22	23	24	25	**26**
26	27	28	29	30	1	2	3

JUNE

MONDAY
13

TUESDAY
14

WEDNESDAY
15

THURSDAY
16

FRIDAY
17

SATURDAY
18

SUNDAY
19
FATHER'S DAY

NOTES

JUNE

	M	T	W	T	F	S	**S**
22	30	31	1	2	3	4	**5**
23	6	7	8	9	10	11	**12**
24	13	14	15	16	17	18	**19**
25	20	21	22	23	24	25	**26**
26	27	28	29	30	1	2	3

JUNE

MONDAY
20 ☼ ○
22:34 UTC

TUESDAY
21

WEDNESDAY
22

THURSDAY
23

FRIDAY
24

SATURDAY
25

SUNDAY
26

NOTES

JUNE

	M	T	W	T	F	S	S
22	30	31	1	2	3	4	**5**
23	6	7	8	9	10	11	**12**
24	13	14	15	16	17	18	**19**
25	20	21	22	23	24	25	**26**
26	27	28	29	30	1	2	3

JUNE–JULY

MONDAY
27 ☾

TUESDAY
28

WEDNESDAY
29

THURSDAY
30

FRIDAY
1

SATURDAY
2

SUNDAY
3

NOTES

JUNE

M	T	W	T	F	S	S
22	30	31	1	2	3	4	**5**
23	6	7	8	9	10	11	**12**
24	13	14	15	16	17	18	**19**
25	20	21	22	23	24	25	**26**
26	27	28	29	30	1	2	3

JULY

MONDAY
4

TUESDAY
5

WEDNESDAY
6
EID AL-FITR

THURSDAY
7

FRIDAY
8

SATURDAY
9

SUNDAY
10

NOTES

JULY

M	T	W	T	F	S	S
26	27	28	29	30	1	2	3
27	4	5	6	7	8	9	10
28	11	12	13	14	15	16	17
29	18	19	20	21	22	23	24
30	25	26	27	28	29	30	31

JULY

MONDAY
11

TUESDAY
12 ☽
BATTLE OF THE BOYNE
(NI)

WEDNESDAY
13

THURSDAY
14

2016

FRIDAY
15
ST SWITHIN'S DAY

SATURDAY
16

SUNDAY
17

NOTES

JULY

	M	T	W	T	F	S	S
26	27	28	29	30	1	2	**3**
27	4	5	6	7	8	9	**10**
28	11	12	13	14	15	16	**17**
29	18	19	20	21	22	23	**24**
30	25	26	27	28	29	30	**31**

JULY

MONDAY
18

TUESDAY
19 ○

WEDNESDAY
20

THURSDAY
21

FRIDAY
22

SATURDAY
23

SUNDAY
24

NOTES

JULY

	M	T	W	T	F	S	**S**
26	27	28	29	30	1	2	**3**
27	4	5	6	7	8	9	**10**
28	11	12	13	14	15	16	**17**
29	18	19	20	21	22	23	**24**
30	25	26	27	28	29	30	**31**

JULY

MONDAY
25

TUESDAY
26 ☾

WEDNESDAY
27

THURSDAY
28

2016

FRIDAY
29

SATURDAY
30

SUNDAY
31

NOTES

	M	T	W	T	F	S	S
26	27	28	29	30	1	2	**3**
27	4	5	6	7	8	9	**10**
28	11	12	13	14	15	16	**17**
29	18	19	20	21	22	23	**24**
30	25	26	27	28	29	30	**31**

AUGUST

MONDAY
1
BANK HOLIDAY (IE, SCOT.)

TUESDAY
2 ●

WEDNESDAY
3

THURSDAY
4

FRIDAY
5

SATURDAY
6

SUNDAY
7

NOTES

AUGUST

	M	T	W	T	F	S	S
31	1	2	3	4	5	6	7
32	8	9	10	11	12	13	14
33	15	16	17	18	19	20	21
34	22	23	24	25	26	27	28
35	29	30	31	1	2	3	4

AUGUST

MONDAY
8

TUESDAY
9

WEDNESDAY
10 ☽

THURSDAY
11

FRIDAY
12

SATURDAY
13

SUNDAY
14

NOTES

AUGUST

	M	T	W	T	F	S	S
31	1	2	3	4	5	6	**7**
32	8	9	10	11	12	13	**14**
33	15	16	17	18	19	20	**21**
34	22	23	24	25	26	27	**28**
35	29	30	31	1	2	3	4

AUGUST

MONDAY
15

TUESDAY
16

WEDNESDAY
17

THURSDAY
18 ○

FRIDAY
19

SATURDAY
20

SUNDAY
21

NOTES

AUGUST

	M	T	W	T	F	S	**S**
31	1	2	3	4	5	6	**7**
32	8	9	10	11	12	13	**14**
33	15	16	17	18	19	20	**21**
34	22	23	24	25	26	27	**28**
35	29	30	31	1	2	3	4

AUGUST

MONDAY
2 2

TUESDAY
23

WEDNESDAY
24

THURSDAY
25 ☾

FRIDAY
26

SATURDAY
27

SUNDAY
28

NOTES

AUGUST

	M	T	W	T	F	S	S
31	1	2	3	4	5	6	**7**
32	8	9	10	11	12	13	**14**
33	15	16	17	18	19	20	**21**
34	22	23	24	25	26	27	**28**
35	29	30	31	1	2	3	4

AUGUST–SEPTEMBER

MONDAY

29

BANK HOLIDAY
  (UK EXCEPT SCOT.)

TUESDAY

30

WEDNESDAY

31

THURSDAY

1 ●

FRIDAY
2

SATURDAY
3

SUNDAY
4

NOTES

SEPTEMBER

	M	T	W	T	F	S	S
35	29	30	31	1	2	3	**4**
36	5	6	7	8	9	10	**11**
37	12	13	14	15	16	17	**18**
38	19	20	21	22	23	24	**25**
39	26	27	28	29	30	1	2

SEPTEMBER

MONDAY
5

TUESDAY
6

WEDNESDAY
7

THURSDAY
8

FRIDAY
9 ☽

SATURDAY
10

SUNDAY
11
EID AL-ADHA

NOTES

SEPTEMBER

	M	T	W	T	F	S	S
35	29	30	31	1	2	3	4
36	5	6	7	8	9	10	11
37	12	13	14	15	16	17	18
38	19	20	21	22	23	24	25
39	26	27	28	29	30	1	2

SEPTEMBER

MONDAY
12

TUESDAY
13

WEDNESDAY
14

THURSDAY
15

2016

FRIDAY
16 ○

SATURDAY
17

SUNDAY
18

NOTES

SEPTEMBER

	M	T	W	T	F	S	S
35	29	30	31	1	2	3	**4**
36	5	6	7	8	9	10	**11**
37	12	13	14	15	16	17	**18**
38	19	20	21	22	23	24	**25**
39	26	27	28	29	30	1	2

SEPTEMBER

MONDAY
19

TUESDAY
20

WEDNESDAY
21

THURSDAY
22
14:21 UTC

2016

FRIDAY
23 ☾

SATURDAY
24

SUNDAY
25

NOTES

	M	T	W	T	F	S	S
35	29	30	31	1	2	3	4
36	5	6	7	8	9	10	11
37	12	13	14	15	16	17	18
38	19	20	21	22	23	24	25
39	26	27	28	29	30	1	2

SEPTEMBER–OCTOBER

MONDAY
26

TUESDAY
27

WEDNESDAY
28

THURSDAY
29

FRIDAY
30

SATURDAY
1 ●

SUNDAY
2
MUHARRAM BEGINS

NOTES

SEPTEMBER

	M	T	W	T	F	S	S
35	29	30	31	1	2	3	**4**
36	5	6	7	8	9	10	**11**
37	12	13	14	15	16	17	**18**
38	19	20	21	22	23	24	**25**
39	**26**	**27**	**28**	**29**	**30**	1	2

OCTOBER

MONDAY
3
ROSH HASHANAH

TUESDAY
4

WEDNESDAY
5

THURSDAY
6

FRIDAY
7

SATURDAY
8

SUNDAY
9 ☽

NOTES

OCTOBER

	M	T	W	T	F	S	S
39	26	27	28	29	30	1	**2**
40	3	4	5	6	7	8	**9**
41	10	11	12	13	14	15	**16**
42	17	18	19	20	21	22	**23**
43	24/31	25	26	27	28	29	**30**

OCTOBER

MONDAY
10

TUESDAY
11

WEDNESDAY
12
YOM KIPPUR

THURSDAY
13

2016

FRIDAY
14

SATURDAY
15

SUNDAY
16 ○

NOTES

OCTOBER

	M	T	W	T	F	S	S
39	26	27	28	29	30	1	**2**
40	3	4	5	6	7	8	**9**
41	10	11	12	13	14	15	**16**
42	17	18	19	20	21	22	**23**
43	24/31	25	26	27	28	29	**30**

OCTOBER

MONDAY
17
SUKKOT

TUESDAY
18

WEDNESDAY
19

THURSDAY
20

FRIDAY
21

SATURDAY
22 ☾

SUNDAY
23

NOTES

OCTOBER

	M	T	W	T	F	S	S
39	26	27	28	29	30	1	**2**
40	3	4	5	6	7	8	**9**
41	10	11	12	13	14	15	**16**
42	17	18	19	20	21	22	**23**
43	24/31	25	26	27	28	29	**30**

OCTOBER

MONDAY
24

TUESDAY
25

WEDNESDAY
26

THURSDAY
27

FRIDAY
28

SATURDAY
29

SUNDAY
30 ● ◔

NOTES

OCTOBER

	M	T	W	T	F	S	S
39	26	27	28	29	30	1	**2**
40	3	4	5	6	7	8	**9**
41	10	11	12	13	14	15	**16**
42	17	18	19	20	21	22	**23**
43	²⁴/₃₁	25	26	27	28	29	**30**

OCTOBER–NOVEMBER

MONDAY
31
HALLOWEEN
BANK HOLIDAY (IE)

TUESDAY
1

WEDNESDAY
2

THURSDAY
3

FRIDAY
4

SATURDAY
5
GUY FAWKES NIGHT

SUNDAY
6
REMEMBRANCE SUNDAY

NOTES

NOVEMBER

	M	T	W	T	F	S	S
44	31	1	2	3	4	5	6
45	7	8	9	10	11	12	13
46	14	15	16	17	18	19	20
47	21	22	23	24	25	26	27
48	28	29	30	1	2	3	4

NOVEMBER

MONDAY
7 ☽

TUESDAY
8

WEDNESDAY
9

THURSDAY
10

FRIDAY
11

SATURDAY
12

SUNDAY
13

NOTES

NOVEMBER

	M	T	W	T	F	S	S
44	31	1	2	3	4	5	**6**
45	7	8	9	10	11	12	**13**
46	14	15	16	17	18	19	**20**
47	21	22	23	24	25	26	**27**
48	28	29	30	1	2	3	4

MONDAY
14 ○

TUESDAY
15

WEDNESDAY
16

THURSDAY
17

FRIDAY
18

SATURDAY
19

SUNDAY
20

NOTES

		NOVEMBER				
	M	T W	T	F	S	S
44	31	1 2	3	4	5	**6**
45	7	8 9	10	11	12	**13**
46	14	15 16	17	18	19	**20**
47	21	22 23	24	25	26	**27**
48	28	29 30	1	2	3	4

NOVEMBER

MONDAY
21 ☾

TUESDAY
22

WEDNESDAY
23

THURSDAY
24

FRIDAY
25

SATURDAY
26

SUNDAY
27

NOTES

NOVEMBER

	M	T	W	T	F	S	S
44	31	1	2	3	4	5	**6**
45	7	8	9	10	11	12	**13**
46	14	15	16	17	18	19	**20**
47	21	22	23	24	25	26	**27**
48	28	29	30	1	2	3	4

NOVEMBER–DECEMBER

MONDAY
28

TUESDAY
29 ●

WEDNESDAY
30
ST ANDREW'S DAY (SCOT.)

THURSDAY
1

FRIDAY
2

SATURDAY
3

SUNDAY
4

NOTES

DECEMBER

	M	T	W	T	F	S	S
48	28	29	30	1	2	3	**4**
49	5	6	7	8	9	10	**11**
50	12	13	14	15	16	17	**18**
51	19	20	21	22	23	24	**25**
52	26	27	28	29	30	31	1

MONDAY
5

TUESDAY
6

WEDNESDAY
7 ☽

THURSDAY
8

FRIDAY
9

SATURDAY
10

SUNDAY
11
MAWLID AL-NABI

NOTES

DECEMBER

	M	T	W	T	F	S	S
48	28	29	30	1	2	3	**4**
49	5	6	7	8	9	10	**11**
50	12	13	14	15	16	17	**18**
51	19	20	21	22	23	24	**25**
52	26	27	28	29	30	31	1

DECEMBER

MONDAY
12

TUESDAY
13

WEDNESDAY
14 ○

THURSDAY
15

FRIDAY
16

SATURDAY
17

SUNDAY
18

NOTES

DECEMBER

	M	T	W	T	F	S	S
48	28	29	30	1	2	3	**4**
49	5	6	7	8	9	10	**11**
50	12	13	14	15	16	17	**18**
51	19	20	21	22	23	24	**25**
52	26	27	28	29	30	31	1

DECEMBER

MONDAY
19

TUESDAY
20

WEDNESDAY
21 ☀ ☾
10:44 UTC

THURSDAY
22

FRIDAY
23

SATURDAY
24

SUNDAY
25
CHRISTMAS DAY
HANUKKAH

NOTES

DECEMBER

	M	T	W	T	F	S	S
48	28	29	30	1	2	3	**4**
49	5	6	7	8	9	10	**11**
50	12	13	14	15	16	17	**18**
51	**19**	**20**	**21**	**22**	**23**	**24**	**25**
52	26	27	28	29	30	31	1

DECEMBER–JANUARY

MONDAY
26
BOXING DAY (UK)
ST STEPHEN'S DAY (IE)

TUESDAY
27

WEDNESDAY
28

THURSDAY
29 ●

FRIDAY
30

SATURDAY
31
NEW YEAR'S EVE
HOGMANAY (SCOT.)

SUNDAY
1
NEW YEAR'S DAY

NOTES

DECEMBER

	M	T	W	T	F	S	S
48	28	29	30	1	2	3	**4**
49	5	6	7	8	9	10	**11**
50	12	13	14	15	16	17	**18**
51	19	20	21	22	23	24	**25**
52	26	27	28	29	30	31	1

INTERNATIONAL HOLIDAYS 2016

ALGERIA

January 1	New Year's Day
May 1	Labour Day
June 6	Ramadan begins
July 5	Independence Day
6	Eid al-Fitr
September 11	Eid al-Adha
October 2	Muharram begins
11	Ashura
November 1	Revolution Day
December 11	Mawlid En Nabaoui Echarif

ARGENTINA

January 1	New Year's Day
February 8	Carnival
March 24	Truth and Justice Memorial Day
25	Good Friday
27	Easter
April 2	Malvinas Day
May 1	Labour Day
25	First Government Day
June 20	Flag Day
July 9	Independence Day
August 15	General San Martín Day
October 12	Day of Respect to Cultural Diversity
November 28	Day of National Sovereignty
December 8	Immaculate Conception
25	Christmas Day

AUSTRALIA

January 1	New Year's Day
26	Australia Day
March 25	Good Friday
26	Easter Saturday*
27	Easter
28	Easter Monday
April 25	Anzac Day
June 13	Queen's Birthday*
December 25	Christmas Day
26	Boxing Day

AUSTRIA

January 1	New Year's Day
6	Epiphany
March 25	Good Friday*
27	Easter
28	Easter Monday
May 1	Labour Day
5	Ascension
16	Whit Monday
26	Corpus Christi Day
August 15	Assumption
October 26	National Day
November 1	All Saints' Day
December 8	Immaculate Conception
25	Christmas Day
26	St Stephen's Day

BELGIUM

January 1	New Year's Day
March 27	Easter
28	Easter Monday
May 1	Labour Day
5	Ascension
16	Whit Monday
July 21	National Day
August 15	Assumption
November 1	All Saints' Day
11	Armistice Day
December 25	Christmas Day

BOLIVIA

January 1	New Year's Day
22	Plurinational State Day
February 8	Carnival
March 25	Good Friday
27	Easter
May 1	Labour Day
26	Corpus Christi Day
June 21	Winter Solstice
July 16	La Paz Day*
August 6	National Day
November 2	All Souls' Day
December 25	Christmas Day

BRAZIL

January 1	New Year's Day
February 8	Carnival
March 25	Good Friday
27	Easter
April 21	Tiradentes Day
May 1	Labour Day

INTERNATIONAL HOLIDAYS 2016

26 Corpus Christi Day
September 7 Independence Day
October 12 Our Lady of Aparecida Day
November 2 All Souls' Day
15 Republic Day
December 25 Christmas Day

BULGARIA
January 1 New Year's Day
March 3 Liberation Day
April 29 Orthodox Good Friday
30 Orthodox Holy Saturday
May 1 Orthodox Easter
Labour Day
2 Orthodox Easter Monday
6 St George's Day
Army Day
24 Culture and Literacy Day
September 6 Unification Day
22 Independence Day
November 1 Revival Leaders' Day*
December 24 Christmas Eve
25 Christmas Day
26 Second Christmas Day
31 New Year's Eve

CANADA
January 1 New Year's Day
February 15 Civic Holiday*
March 25 Good Friday
27 Easter
May 23 Victoria Day
July 1 Canada Day
August 1 Civic Holiday*
September 5 Labour Day
October 10 Thanksgiving Day
November 11 Remembrance Day
December 25 Christmas Day
26 Boxing Day

CHILE
January 1 New Year's Day
March 25 Good Friday
26 Holy Saturday
27 Easter
May 1 Labour Day
21 Navy Day

June 29 St Peter and St Paul's Day
July 16 Our Lady of Carmen Day
August 15 Assumption
September 18 Independence Day
19 Army Day
October 12 Columbus Day
31 Reformation Day
November 1 All Saints' Day
December 8 Immaculate Conception
25 Christmas Day
31 New Year's Eve*

CHINA
January 1 New Year's Day
February 8 Chinese New Year
April 4 Tomb Sweeping Day
May 1 Labour Day
June 9 Dragon Boat Festival
September 15 Mid-Autumn Festival
October 1 National Day

COLOMBIA
January 1 New Year's Day
6 Epiphany
March 19 St Joseph's Day
24 Maundy Thursday
25 Good Friday
27 Easter
May 1 Labour Day
9 Ascension
30 Corpus Christi Day
June 6 Sacred Heart Day
29 St Peter and St Paul's Day
July 20 Independence Day
August 7 Battle of Boyacá Day
15 Assumption
October 12 Columbus Day
November 1 All Saints' Day
11 Cartagena Independence Day
December 8 Immaculate Conception
25 Christmas Day

COSTA RICA
January 1 New Year's Day
March 24 Maundy Thursday
25 Good Friday
27 Easter

INTERNATIONAL HOLIDAYS 2016

April 11 Juan Santamaria Day
May 1 Labour Day
July 25 Guanacaste Day
August 2 Lady of the Angels' Day
15 Mothers' Day
Assumption
September 15 Independence Day
October 12 Columbus Day
December 25 Christmas Day

CROATIA

January 1 New Year's Day
6 Epiphany
March 27 Easter
28 Easter Monday
May 1 Labour Day
26 Corpus Christi Day
June 22 Anti-Fascism Day
25 Statehood Day
August 5 Victory and Homeland
Thanksgiving Day
15 Assumption
October 8 Independence Day
November 1 All Saints' Day
December 25 Christmas Day
26 St Stephen's Day

CUBA

January 1 Liberation Day
2 New Year Public Holiday
March 25 Good Friday
May 1 Labour Day
July 25 Revolution Anniversary
October 10 War of Independence
Anniversary
December 25 Christmas Day
31 End of the Year Public Holiday

CZECH REPUBLIC

January 1 New Year's Day
March 27 Easter
28 Easter Monday
May 1 May Day
8 Liberation Day
July 5 St Cyril and St Methodius Day
6 Jan Hus Day
September 28 Statehood Day

October 28 Independence Day
November 17 Freedom and Democracy Day
December 24 Christmas Eve
25 Christmas Day
26 Second Christmas Day

DENMARK

January 1 New Year's Day
March 24 Maundy Thursday
25 Good Friday
27 Easter
28 Easter Monday
April 22 Prayer Day
May 5 Ascension
15 Whitsun
16 Whit Monday
June 5 Constitution Day
December 24 Christmas Eve
25 Christmas Day
26 Second Christmas Day
31 New Year's Eve

DOMINICAN REPUBLIC

January 1 New Year's Day
6 Epiphany
21 Our Lady of Altagracia Day
26 Juan Pablo Duarte Day
February 27 Independence Day
March 25 Good Friday
27 Easter
May 1 Labour Day
26 Corpus Christi Day
August 16 Restoration Day
September 24 Our Lady of Mercedes Day
November 6 Constitution Day
December 25 Christmas Day

ECUADOR

January 1 New Year's Day
February 8 Carnival
March 25 Good Friday
27 Easter
May 1 Labour Day
24 Battle of Pichincha Day
July 25 Guayaquil Day*
August 10 National Day

INTERNATIONAL HOLIDAYS 2016

October 9 Guayaquil Independence Day
November 2 All Souls' Day
3 Cuenca Independence Day
December 6 Quito Day*
25 Christmas Day
31 New Year's Eve*

EGYPT

January 7 Coptic Christmas
25 Revolution Day
April 25 Sinai Liberation Day
May 1 Coptic Easter
Labour Day
2 Sham el-Nessim
June 6 Ramadan begins
July 6 Iftar Bayram
23 National Day
September 10 Eid al-Adha
October 2 Muharram begins
6 Armed Forces Day
December 11 Mawlid al-Nabi

ESTONIA

January 1 New Year's Day
February 24 Independence Day
March 25 Good Friday
27 Easter
May 1 May Day
15 Pentecost
June 23 Victory Day
24 Midsummer's Day
St John's Day
August 20 Restoration of Independence
Day
December 24 Christmas Eve
25 Christmas Day
26 Boxing Day

FINLAND

January 1 New Year's Day
6 Epiphany
March 25 Good Friday
27 Easter
28 Easter Monday
May 1 May Day
5 Ascension
15 Pentecost

June 25 Midsummer's Day
November 5 All Saints' Day
December 6 Independence Day
25 Christmas Day
26 Second Christmas Day

FRANCE

January 1 New Year's Day
March 27 Easter
28 Easter Monday
May 1 Labour Day
5 Ascension
8 WWII Victory Day
16 Whit Monday
July 14 National Day
August 15 Assumption
November 1 All Saints' Day
11 Armistice Day
December 25 Christmas Day

GEORGIA

January 1 New Year's Day
7 Orthodox Christmas Day
19 Orthodox Epiphany
March 3 Mothers' Day
8 International Women's Day
21 Nowruz
April 9 Restoration of Independence
Day
29 Orthodox Good Friday
30 Orthodox Holy Saturday
May 1 Orthodox Easter
2 Orthodox Easter Monday
Memorial Day
9 Victory Day
12 St Andrew's Day
26 Independence Day
August 28 Day of the Virgin Mary
October 14 Georgian Orthodox Festival
November 23 St George's Day

GERMANY

January 1 New Year's Day
March 25 Good Friday
27 Easter
28 Easter Monday
May 1 Labour Day

INTERNATIONAL HOLIDAYS 2016

5 Ascension
16 Whit Monday
October 3 Day of German Unity
December 25 Christmas Day
26 Second Christmas Day

GREECE

January 1 New Year's Day
6 Epiphany
March 14 Shrove Monday
25 Independence Day
April 29 Orthodox Good Friday
May 1 Orthodox Easter
Labour Day
2 Orthodox Easter Monday
June 19 Orthodox Whit Sunday
20 Orthodox Whit Monday
August 15 Assumption
October 28 National Day
December 25 Christmas Day
26 Second Christmas Day

GUATEMALA

January 1 New Year's Day
March 24 Maundy Thursday
25 Good Friday
26 Holy Saturday
27 Easter
May 1 Labour Day
June 30 Army Day
July 1 July Bank Holiday*
August 15 Assumption*
September 15 Independence Day
October 20 Revolution Day
November 1 All Saints' Day
December 24 Christmas Eve
25 Christmas Day
31 New Year's Eve

HONDURAS

January 1 New Year's Day
February 3 Virgin of Suyapa Day
March 21 Government Holiday
24 Maundy Thursday
25 Good Friday
26 Holy Saturday
27 Easter

April 14 Americas' Day Holiday
May 1 Labour Day
September 15 Independence Day
October 3 General Francisco Morazán's Birthday
12 Columbus Day
21 Armed Forces Day
December 25 Christmas Day

HUNGARY

January 1 New Year's Day
March 15 1848 Revolution Day
27 Easter
28 Easter Monday
May 1 Labour Day
16 Whit Monday
August 20 National Day
October 23 Republic Day
November 1 All Saints' Day
December 25 Christmas Day
26 Second Christmas Day

ICELAND

January 1 New Year's Day
March 24 Maundy Thursday
25 Good Friday
27 Easter
28 Easter Monday
April 21 First Day of Summer
May 1 Labour Day
5 Ascension
15 Whitsun
16 Whit Monday
June 17 Independence Day
August 1 Commerce Day
December 24 Christmas Eve
25 Christmas Day
26 Boxing Day
31 New Year's Eve

INDIA

January 26 Republic Day
March 7 Maha Shivaratri
23 Holi
25 Good Friday
April 19 Mahavir Jayanti
May 1 May Day

INTERNATIONAL HOLIDAYS 2016

21 Buddha Purnima
July 6 Eid al-Fitr
August 15 Independence Day
25 Janmashtami
September 11 Bakri Id/Idu'l Zuha
October 2 Mahatma Gandhi's Birthday
11 Muharram begins
Dussehra
30 Diwali
November 14 Guru Nanak's Birthday
December 11 Mawlid al-Nabi
25 Christmas Day

IRAN

February 11 Anniversary of the
Islamic Revolution
March 12 Martyrdom of Hazart Fatemesh
19 Oil Nationalisation Day
20 Nowruz
31 Islamic Republic Day
April 1 Sizdehbedar
20 Imam Ali's Birthday
May 4 Mabaath
22 Imam Mahdi's Birthday
June 3 Demise of Imam Khomeini
4 15th Khordad National Uprising
(1963)
26 Martyrdom of Imam Ali
July 6 Eid al-Fitr
30 Martyrdom of Imam Sadeq
September 11 Eid-e-Qorban
19 Eid-e-Ghadir
October 10 Tasua
11 Ashura
November 20 Arba'in-e Hosseini
28 Death of Prophet Mohammad
Martyrdom of Imam Hasan
29 Martyrdom of Imam Reza
December 16 Birth of Prophet Mohammad
and of Imam Sadegh

ISRAEL

March 24 Purim
April 23 Passover
May 12 Independence Day
June 12 Shavuot
August 13 Tisha B'Av

October 3 Rosh Hashanah
12 Yom Kippur
17 Sukkot
24 Simchat Torah

ITALY

January 1 New Year's Day
6 Epiphany
March 27 Easter
28 Easter Monday
April 25 Liberation Day
May 1 Labour Day
June 2 Republic Day
August 15 Assumption
November 1 All Saints' Day
December 8 Immaculate Conception
25 Christmas Day
26 St Stephen's Day

JAPAN

January 1 New Year's Day
11 Coming of Age Day
February 11 National Foundation Day
March 21 Spring Equinox
April 29 Showa Day
May 3 Constitution Memorial Day
4 Greenery Day
5 Children's Day
July 18 Marine Day
August 11 Mountain Day
September 19 Respect for the Aged Day
22 Autumn Equinox
October 10 Sports Day
November 3 Culture Day
23 Labour Thanksgiving Day
December 23 Emperor's Birthday

JORDAN

January 1 New Year's Day
May 1 Labour Day
25 Independence Day
June 6 Ramadan begins
July 6 Eid al-Fitr
September 11 Eid al-Adha
October 2 Muharram begins
December 11 Mawlid al-Nabi
25 Christmas Day

INTERNATIONAL HOLIDAYS 2016

LATVIA

January 1	New Year's Day
March 25	Good Friday
27	Easter
28	Easter Monday
May 1	Labour Day
4	Declaration of Independence Day
June 23	Midsummer's Eve
24	St John's Day
November 18	Proclamation of the Republic
December 24	Christmas Eve
25	Christmas Day
26	Second Christmas Day
31	New Year's Eve

LITHUANIA

January 1	New Year's Day
February 16	Independence Day
March 11	Restoration of Independence Day
27	Easter
28	Easter Monday
May 1	Labour Day
	Mothers' Day
June 5	Fathers' Day
24	St John's Day
July 6	Statehood Day
August 15	Assumption
November 1	All Saints' Day
December 24	Christmas Eve
25	Christmas Day
26	Second Christmas Day

LUXEMBOURG

January 1	New Year's Day
February 8	Carnival
March 25	Good Friday
27	Easter
28	Easter Monday
May 1	Labour Day
5	Ascension
16	Whit Monday
June 23	National Day
August 15	Assumption
September 5	Luxembourg City Fête*

November 1	All Saints' Day
December 24	Christmas Eve
25	Christmas Day
26	St Stephen's Day

MACEDONIA

January 1	New Year's Day
6	Orthodox Christmas Eve
7	Orthodox Christmas Day
April 29	Orthodox Good Friday
May 1	Orthodox Easter
	Labour Day
2	Orthodox Easter Monday
24	St Cyril and St Methodius Day
July 6	Ramazan Bajram
August 2	Republic Day
September 8	Independence Day
11	Kurban Bajram
October 11	Uprising Against Fascism Day
23	Revolutionary Struggle Day
December 8	St Clement of Ohrid Day

MALTA

January 1	New Year's Day
February 10	Feast of St Paul's Shipwreck
March 19	St Joseph's Day
25	Good Friday
27	Easter
31	Freedom Day
May 1	Workers' Day
June 7	Sette Giugno
29	St Peter and St Paul's Day
August 15	Assumption
September 8	Feast of Our Lady of Victories
21	Independence Day
December 8	Immaculate Conception
13	Republic Day
25	Christmas Day

MEXICO

January 1	New Year's Day
February 1	Constitution Day
March 21	Benito Juárez Day
25	Good Friday*
27	Easter
May 1	Labour Day

INTERNATIONAL HOLIDAYS 2016

September 16 Independence Day
November 21 Revolution Day
December 25 Christmas Day

MOROCCO

January 1 New Year's Day
11 Independence Manifesto Day
(1944)
May 1 Labour Day
June 6 Ramadan begins
July 6 Eid al-Fitr
30 Throne Day
August 14 Oued Ed-Dahab Day
20 Revolution Day (1953)
21 HM Mohammed VI's Birthday
September 11 Eid al-Adha
October 2 Muharram begins
November 6 Green March Day
18 Independence Day
December 11 Mawlid al-Nabi

NETHERLANDS

January 1 New Year's Day
March 25 Good Friday*
27 Easter
28 Easter Monday
April 27 King's Birthday
May 5 Liberation Day
Ascension
15 Pentecost
16 Whit Monday
December 25 Christmas Day
26 Second Christmas Day

NEW ZEALAND

January 1 New Year's Day
2 Second Day of New Year
February 6 Waitangi Day
March 25 Good Friday
27 Easter
28 Easter Monday
April 25 Anzac Day
June 6 Queen's Birthday
October 24 Labour Day
December 25 Christmas Day
26 Boxing Day

NORWAY

January 1 New Year's Day
March 24 Maundy Thursday
25 Good Friday
27 Easter
28 Easter Monday
May 1 Labour Day
5 Ascension
15 Whitsun
16 Whit Monday
17 Constitution Day
December 25 Christmas Day
26 Second Christmas Day

PARAGUAY

January 1 New Year's Day
March 1 National Heroes' Day
24 Maundy Thursday
25 Good Friday
27 Easter
May 1 Labour Day
14 Start of Independence
15 Independence Day
June 12 Chaco Armistice Day
August 15 Founding of Asunción
September 29 Battle of Boquerón Day
December 8 Virgin of Caacupé Day
25 Christmas Day
31 New Year's Eve

PERU

January 1 New Year's Day
March 24 Maundy Thursday
25 Good Friday
27 Easter
May 1 Labour Day
June 29 St Peter and St Paul's Day
July 28 Independence Day
August 30 Saint Rose of Lima Day
October 8 Battle of Angamos Day
November 1 All Saints' Day
December 8 Immaculate Conception
25 Christmas Day

POLAND

January 1 New Year's Day

INTERNATIONAL HOLIDAYS 2016

6 Epiphany
March 27 Easter
28 Easter Monday
May 1 State Holiday
3 Constitution Day
15 Pentecost
26 Corpus Christi Day
August 15 Assumption
November 1 All Saints' Day
11 Independence Day
December 25 Christmas Day
26 Second Christmas Day

PORTUGAL

January 1 New Year's Day
February 9 Shrove Tuesday (Carnival)
March 25 Good Friday
27 Easter
April 25 Liberation Day
May 1 Labour Day
26 Corpus Christi Day
June 10 National Day
August 15 Assumption
October 5 Republic Day
November 1 All Saints' Day
December 1 Independence Day
8 Immaculate Conception
25 Christmas Day

PUERTO RICO

January 1 New Year's Day
6 Epiphany
11 Eugenio María de Hostos' Day
18 Martin Luther King Jr Day
February 15 Presidents' Day
March 22 Emancipation Day
25 Good Friday
27 Easter
April 18 José de Diego Day
May 30 Memorial Day
July 4 Independence Day
18 Luis Muñoz Rivera Day
25 Constitution Day
27 José Celso Barbosa's Birthday
September 5 Labour Day
October 12 Columbus Day

November 8 Public Holiday
(General Election)
11 Veterans' Day
19 Puerto Rico Discovery Day
24 Thanksgiving Day
December 24 Christmas Eve
25 Christmas Day

QATAR

January 1 New Year's Day
February 9 National Sports Day
March 6 Bank Holiday
July 6 Eid al-Fitr
September 10 Eid al-Adha
December 18 National Day

ROMANIA

January 1 New Year's Day
2 Second Day of New Year
May 1 Orthodox Easter
Labour Day
2 Orthodox Easter Monday
June 19 Pentecost
August 15 Assumption
November 30 St Andrew's Day
December 1 National Day
25 Christmas Day
26 Second Christmas Day

RUSSIA

January 1 New Year's Day
7 Orthodox Christmas Day
February 23 Defenders' Day
March 8 International Women's Day
May 1 Orthodox Easter
Labour Day
9 Victory Day
June 12 Russia Day
November 4 Unity Day

SAUDI ARABIA

June 6 Ramadan begins
July 6 Eid al-Fitr
September 10 Eid al-Adha
23 National Day
October 2 Muharram begins
11 Ashura
December 11 Mawlid al-Nabi

INTERNATIONAL HOLIDAYS 2016

SLOVAKIA

January 1	New Year's Day
	Republic Day
6	Epiphany
March 25	Good Friday
27	Easter
28	Easter Monday
May 1	May Day
8	Victory Day
July 5	St Cyril and St Methodius Day
August 29	Slovak National Uprising Day
September 1	Constitution Day
15	Our Lady of Sorrows Day
November 1	All Saints' Day
17	Freedom and Democracy Day
December 24	Christmas Eve
25	Christmas Day
26	Boxing Day

SLOVENIA

January 1	New Year's Day
February 8	Culture Day
March 27	Easter
28	Easter Monday
April 27	Resistance Day
May 1	Labour Day
June 25	National Day
August 15	Assumption
October 31	Reformation Day
November 1	All Saints' Day
December 25	Christmas Day
26	Independence Day

SOUTH AFRICA

January 1	New Year's Day
March 21	Human Rights Day
25	Good Friday
27	Easter
28	Easter Monday
	Family Day
April 27	Freedom Day
May 1	Workers' Day
June 16	Youth Day
August 9	National Women's Day
September 24	Heritage Day
December 16	Day of Reconciliation

25	Christmas Day
26	Day of Goodwill

SOUTH KOREA

January 1	New Year's Day
February 7	Lunar New Year
March 1	Declaration of Independence Day
April 13	Public Holiday (Parliamentary Elections)
May 1	Labour Day
5	Children's Day
14	Buddha's Birthday
June 6	Memorial Day
August 15	Liberation Day
September 14	Harvest Moon Festival
October 3	National Foundation Day
9	Hangul Day
December 25	Christmas Day

SPAIN

January 1	New Year's Day
6	Epiphany
March 24	Maundy Thursday*
25	Good Friday
27	Easter
May 1	Labour Day
August 15	Assumption
October 12	National Day
November 1	All Saints' Day
December 6	Constitution Day
8	Immaculate Conception
25	Christmas Day
26	St Stephen's Day*

SWEDEN

January 1	New Year's Day
6	Epiphany
March 25	Good Friday
27	Easter
28	Easter Monday
May 1	Labour Day
5	Ascension
15	Pentecost
June 6	National Day
25	Midsummer's Day
November 5	All Saints' Day

INTERNATIONAL HOLIDAYS 2016

December 25 Christmas Day
26 Second Christmas Day

SWITZERLAND

January 1 New Year's Day
March 25 Good Friday*
27 Easter
28 Easter Monday*
May 1 Labour Day*
5 Ascension
16 Whit Monday*
August 1 National Day
December 25 Christmas Day
26 St Stephen's Day*

SYRIA

January 1 New Year's Day
March 8 Revolution Day
21 Mothers' Day
27 Easter
April 17 Independence Day
May 1 Orthodox Easter
Labour Day
6 Martyrs' Day
June 6 Ramadan begins
July 6 Eid al-Fitr
September 11 Eid al-Adha
October 2 Muharram begins
6 Tishreen Liberation War Day
December 11 Mawlid al-Nabi
25 Christmas Day

TUNISIA

January 1 New Year's Day
14 Revolution and Youth Day
March 20 Independence Day
April 9 Martyrs' Day
May 1 Labour Day
June 6 Ramadan begins
July 6 Eid al-Fitr
25 Republic Day
August 13 Women's Day
September 11 Eid al-Adha
October 2 Muharram begins
15 Evacuation Day
December 11 Mawlid al-Nabi

TURKEY

January 1 New Year's Day

April 23 National Sovereignty and
Children's Day
May 1 Labour and Solidarity Day
19 Atatürk Day
Youth and Sports Day
July 5 Ramazan Bayramy Eve
6 Ramazan Bayramy
August 30 Victory Day
September 10 Kurban Bayramy Eve
11 Kurban Bayramy
October 29 National Day

UKRAINE

January 1 New Year's Day
7 Orthodox Christmas Day
March 8 International Women's Day
May 1 Orthodox Easter
Labour Day
9 Victory Day
June 19 Orthodox Pentecost
28 Constitution Day
July 6 Uraza Bairam*
August 24 Independence Day
September 11 Qurban Bayram*

UNITED ARAB EMIRATES

January 1 New Year's Day
May 4 Lailat al-Miraj
June 6 Ramadan begins
July 6 Eid al-Fitr
September 10 Eid al-Adha
October 2 Muharram begins
December 2 National Day
11 Mawlid al-Nabi

URUGUAY

January 1 New Year's Day
6 Epiphany
February 8 Carnival
March 21 Holy Week/Tourism Week
24 Maundy Thursday
25 Good Friday
27 Easter
April 19 Landing of the 33 Patriots Day
May 1 Labour Day
18 Battle of Las Piedras Day

INTERNATIONAL HOLIDAYS 2016

June 19 José Artigas' Birthday
July 18 Constitution Day
August 25 Independence Day
October 12 Sarandí Battle Day
November 2 All Souls' Day
December 25 Christmas Day

USA

January 1 New Year's Day
18 Martin Luther King Jr Day
February 15 Presidents' Day
March 27 Easter
May 30 Memorial Day
July 4 Independence Day
September 5 Labour Day
October 10 Columbus Day
November 11 Veterans' Day
24 Thanksgiving Day
December 25 Christmas Day

VENEZUELA

January 1 New Year's Day
6 Epiphany
February 8 Carnival
March 19 St Joseph's Day*
24 Maundy Thursday
25 Good Friday
27 Easter
April 19 Declaration of Independence Day
May 1 Labour Day
9 Ascension
30 Corpus Christi Day

June 24 Battle of Carabobo Day
29 St Peter and St Paul's Day
July 5 Independence Day
24 Simón Bolívar Day
August 15 Assumption
October 12 Indigenous Resistance Day
November 1 All Saints' Day
December 8 Immaculate Conception
24 Christmas Eve
25 Christmas Day

ISLAMIC HOLIDAYS

May 4 Lailat al-Miraj
22 Lailat al-Bara'ah
June 6 Ramadan begins
July 2 Lailat al-Qadr
6 Eid al-Fitr
September 10 Arafat Day
11 Eid al-Adha
October 2 Muharram begins
11 Ashura
December 11 Mawlid al-Nabi
31 New Year's Eve

JEWISH HOLIDAYS

March 24 Purim
April 23 Passover
June 12 Shavuot
October 3 Rosh Hashanah
12 Yom Kippur
17 Sukkot
December 25 Hanukkah

*Not a public holiday/Not a public holiday in all regions.
This table lists commemorative dates. Additional public holidays may precede or follow some dates.
Regional holidays may not be included. This information is provided as a guide only.

NOTES

2017

JANUARY

M	T	W	T	F	S	S
26	27	28	29	30	31	**1**
2	3	4	5	6	7	**8**
9	10	11	12	13	14	**15**
16	17	18	19	20	21	**22**
23/30 24/31	25	26	27	28	**29**	

FEBRUARY

M	T	W	T	F	S	S
30	31	1	2	3	4	**5**
6	7	8	9	10	11	**12**
13	14	15	16	17	18	**19**
20	21	22	23	24	25	**26**
27	28	1	2	3	4	5

MARCH

M	T	W	T	F	S	S
27	28	1	2	3	4	**5**
6	7	8	9	10	11	**12**
13	14	15	16	17	18	**19**
20	21	22	23	24	25	**26**
27	28	29	30	31	1	2

APRIL

M	T	W	T	F	S	S
27	28	29	30	31	1	**2**
3	4	5	6	7	8	**9**
10	11	12	13	14	15	**16**
17	18	19	20	21	22	**23**
24	25	26	27	28	29	**30**

MAY

M	T	W	T	F	S	S
1	2	3	4	5	6	**7**
8	9	10	11	12	13	**14**
15	16	17	18	19	20	**21**
22	23	24	25	26	27	**28**
29	30	31	1	2	3	4

JUNE

M	T	W	T	F	S	S
29	30	31	1	2	3	**4**
5	6	7	8	9	10	**11**
12	13	14	15	16	17	**18**
19	20	21	22	23	24	**25**
26	27	28	29	30	1	2

JULY

M	T	W	T	F	S	S
26	27	28	29	30	1	**2**
3	4	5	6	7	8	**9**
10	11	12	13	14	15	**16**
17	18	19	20	21	22	**23**
24/31	25	26	27	28	29	**30**

AUGUST

M	T	W	T	F	S	S
31	1	2	3	4	5	**6**
7	8	9	10	11	12	**13**
14	15	16	17	18	19	**20**
21	22	23	24	25	26	**27**
28	29	30	31	1	2	3

SEPTEMBER

M	T	W	T	F	S	S
28	29	30	31	1	2	**3**
4	5	6	7	8	9	**10**
11	12	13	14	15	16	**17**
18	19	20	21	22	23	**24**
25	26	27	28	29	30	1

OCTOBER

M	T	W	T	F	S	S
25	26	27	28	29	30	**1**
2	3	4	5	6	7	**8**
9	10	11	12	13	14	**15**
16	17	18	19	20	21	**22**
23/30 24/31	25	26	27	28	**29**	

NOVEMBER

M	T	W	T	F	S	S
30	31	1	2	3	4	**5**
6	7	8	9	10	11	**12**
13	14	15	16	17	18	**19**
20	21	22	23	24	25	**26**
27	28	29	30	1	2	3

DECEMBER

M	T	W	T	F	S	S
27	28	29	30	1	2	**3**
4	5	6	7	8	9	**10**
11	12	13	14	15	16	**17**
18	19	20	21	22	23	**24**
25	26	27	28	29	30	**31**

HOLIDAYS & CELEBRATIONS 2017

JANUARY

Sunday 1 New Year's Day
Monday 2 Second of January (Scot.)
Saturday 28 Chinese New Year

FEBRUARY

Tuesday 14 Valentine's Day
Tuesday 28 Shrove Tuesday
Pancake Day

MARCH

Wednesday 1 Ash Wednesday
St David's Day
Sunday 5 St Piran's Day
Sunday 12 Purim*
Friday 17 St Patrick's Day (IE, NI)
Sunday 26 Mother's Day

APRIL

Saturday 1 April Fools' Day
Sunday 9 Palm Sunday
Tuesday 11 Passover*
Friday 14 Good Friday (UK)
Sunday 16 Easter
Monday 17 Easter Monday
(except Scot.)
Sunday 23 St George's Day

MAY

Monday 1 Bank Holiday
May Day
Saturday 27 Ramadan begins
Monday 29 Bank Holiday (UK)
Wednesday 31 Shavuot

JUNE

Sunday 4 Whitsun

Monday 5 Bank Holiday (IE)
Sunday 18 Father's Day
Sunday 25 Eid al-Fitr*

JULY

Wednesday 12 Battle of the Boyne (NI)
Saturday 15 St Swithin's Day

AUGUST

Monday 7 Bank Holiday (IE, Scot.)
Monday 28 Bank Holiday
(UK except Scot.)

SEPTEMBER

Friday 1 Eid al-Adha*
Thursday 21 Muharram begins
Rosh Hashanah*
Saturday 30 Yom Kippur

OCTOBER

Thursday 5 Sukkot*
Monday 30 Bank Holiday (IE)
Tuesday 31 Halloween

NOVEMBER

Sunday 5 Remembrance Sunday
Guy Fawkes Night
Thursday 30 Mawlid al-Nabi
St Andrew's Day (Scot.)

DECEMBER

Wednesday 13 Hanukkah*
Monday 25 Christmas Day
Tuesday 26 Boxing Day (UK)
St Stephen's Day (IE)
Sunday 31 New Year's Eve
Hogmanay (Scot.)*

Additional public holidays may precede or follow this date.

NOTES

2017 YEAR PLANNER

	JANUARY	FEBRUARY	MARCH
1	S New Year's Day	W	W Ash Wednesday / St David's Day
2	M Second of January (Scot.)	T	T
3	T	F	F
4	W	S	S
5	T	S	S St Piran's Day
6	F	M	M
7	S	T	T
8	S	W	W
9	M	T	T
10	T	F	F
11	W	S	S
12	T	S	S Purim
13	F	M	M
14	S	T Valentine's Day	T
15	S	W	W
16	M	T	T
17	T	F	F St Patrick's Day (IE, NI)
18	W	S	S
19	T	S	S
20	F	M	M 🏵
21	S	T	T
22	S	W	W
23	M	T	T
24	T	F	F
25	W	S	S
26	T	S	S Mother's Day ☺
27	F	M	M
28	S Chinese New Year	T Shrove Tuesday / Pancake Day	T
29	S		W
30	M		T
31	T		F

2017 YEAR PLANNER

	APRIL		MAY		JUNE	
1	S	April Fools' Day	M	Bank Holiday May Day	T	
2	S		T		F	
3	M		W		S	
4	T		T		S	Whitsun
5	W		F		M	Bank Holiday (IE)
6	T		S		T	
7	F		S		W	
8	S		M		T	
9	S	Palm Sunday	T		F	
10	M		W		S	
11	T	Passover	T		S	
12	W		F		M	
13	T		S		T	
14	F	Good Friday (UK)	S		W	
15	S		M		T	
16	S	Easter	T		F	
17	M	Easter Monday (except Scot.)	W		S	
18	T		T		S	Father's Day
19	W		F		M	
20	T		S		T	
21	F		S		W	
22	S		M		T	
23	S	St George's Day	T		F	
24	M		W		S	
25	T		T		S	Eid al-Fitr
26	W		F		M	
27	T		S	Ramadan begins	T	
28	F		S		W	
29	S		M	Bank Holiday (UK)	T	
30	S		T		F	
31			W	Shavuot		

2017 YEAR PLANNER

	JULY	AUGUST	SEPTEMBER
1	S	T	F — Eid al-Adha
2	S	W	S
3	M	T	S
4	T	F	M
5	W	S	T
6	T	S	W
7	F	M — Bank Holiday (IE, Scot.)	T
8	S	T	F
9	S	W	S
10	M	T	S
11	T	F	M
12	W — Battle of the Boyne (NI)	S	T
13	T	S	W
14	F	M	T
15	S — St Swithin's Day	T	F
16	S	W	S
17	M	T	S
18	T	F	M
19	W	S	T
20	T	S	W
21	F	M	T — Muharram begins / Rosh Hashanah
22	S	T	F
23	S	W	S
24	M	T	S
25	T	F	M
26	W	S	T
27	T	S	W
28	F	M — Bank Holiday (UK except Scot.)	T
29	S	T	F
30	S	W	S — Yom Kippur
31	M	T	

2017 YEAR PLANNER

	OCTOBER	NOVEMBER	DECEMBER
1	S	W	F
2	M	T	S
3	T	F	S
4	W	S	M
5	T — Sukkot	S — Remembrance Sunday / Guy Fawkes Night	T
6	F	M	W
7	S	T	T
8	S	W	F
9	M	T	S
10	T	F	S
11	W	S	M
12	T	S	T
13	F	M	W — Hanukkah
14	S	T	T
15	S	W	F
16	M	T	S
17	T	F	S
18	W	S	M
19	T	S	T
20	F	M	W
21	S	T	T ✳
22	S	W	F
23	M	T	S
24	T	F	S
25	W	S	M — Christmas Day
26	T	S	T — Boxing Day (UK) / St Stephen's Day (IE)
27	F	M	W
28	S	T	T
29	S ☺	W	F
30	M — Bank Holiday (IE)	T — Mawlid al-Nabi / St Andrew's Day (Scot.)	S
31	T — Halloween		S — New Year's Eve / Hogmanay (Scot.)

INTERNATIONAL DIALLING CODES

COUNTRY/AREA	DIAL OUT (ACCESS CODE)	DIAL IN (COUNTRY CODE)	EMERG. NUMBER	COUNTRY/AREA	DIAL OUT (ACCESS CODE)	DIAL IN (COUNTRY CODE)	EMERG. NUMBER
Algeria	00	213	17	Korea (South)	001*	82	999
Argentina	00	54	101	Latvia	00	371	112
Australia	0011	61	000	Lithuania	00	370	112
Austria	00	43	112	Luxembourg	00	352	112
Belgium	00	32	112	Macedonia	00	389	112
Bermuda	011	1441	911	Malaysia	00	60	999
Bolivia	00	591	110	Malta	00	356	112
Brazil	00	55	190	Mexico	00	52	066
Bulgaria	00	359	112	Morocco	00	212	19
Canada	011	1	911	Netherlands	00	31	112
Chile	00	56	133	New Zealand	00	64	111
China	00	86	110	Norway	00	47	112
Colombia	009*	57	112	Pakistan	00	92	15
Costa Rica	00	506	911	Paraguay	00	595	911
Croatia	00	385	112	Peru	00	51	105
Cuba	119	53	106	Philippines	00	63	117
Czech Republic	00	420	112	Poland	00	48	112
Denmark	00	45	112	Portugal	00	351	112
Dominican Repub.	011	1809	911	Puerto Rico	011	1787*	911
Ecuador	00	593	911	Qatar	00	974	999
Egypt	00	20	122	Romania	00	40	112
Estonia	00	372	112	Russia	810	7	112
Finland	00*	358	112	Saudi Arabia	00	966	999
France	00	33	112	Slovakia	00	421	112
Georgia	00	995	112	Slovenia	00	386	112
Germany	00	49	112	South Africa	00	27	10111
Greece	00	30	112	Spain	00	34	112
Guatemala	00	502	110	Sweden	00	46	112
Honduras	00	504	199	Switzerland	00	41	112
Hong Kong	001	852	999	Syria	00	963	112
Hungary	00	36	112	Taiwan	002	886	119
Iceland	00	354	112	Thailand	001	66	191
India	00	91	100	Tunisia	00	216	197
Iran	00	98	110	Turkey	00	90	155
Ireland (Republic)	00	353	112	U.A.E.	00	971	999
Israel	00*	972	100	Ukraine	00	380	112
Italy	00	39	112	United Kingdom	00	44	112
Jamaica	011	1876	119	United States	011	1	911
Japan	010	81	110	Uruguay	00	598	911
Jordan	00	962	911	Venezuela	00	58	171

Additional access codes also in use.

WORLD TIME ZONES

UTC 12:00	UTC+1 13:00	UTC+2 14:00	UTC+3 15:00
Accra	Berlin	Athens	Baghdad
Lisbon	Paris	Cairo	Nairobi
London	Rome	Tel Aviv	Riyadh

UTC+4 16:00	UTC+5 17:00	UTC+5.5 17:30	UTC+6 18:00
Dubai	Karachi	Delhi	Almaty
Moscow	Tashkent	Kolkata	Dhaka
		Mumbai	

UTC+7 19:00	UTC+8 20:00	UTC+9 21:00	UTC+10 22:00
Bangkok	Beijing	Seoul	Melbourne
Jakarta	Manila	Tokyo	Sydney
	Singapore		

UTC+12 24:00	UTC−10 02:00	UTC−9 03:00	UTC−8 04:00
Auckland	Honolulu	Anchorage	Los Angeles
Suva			San Francisco
Wellington			Vancouver

UTC−6 06:00	UTC−5 07:00	UTC−4 08:00	UTC−3 09:00
Chicago	Miami	Halifax	Buenos Aires
Houston	New York	La Paz	Rio de Janeiro
Mexico City	Toronto	Santiago	

Coordinated Universal Time (UTC) is equivalent to Greenwich Mean Time (GMT).

CONVERSIONS

CLOTHING SIZES

WOMEN – CLOTHING							
France/Spain	34	36	38	40	42	44	46
Germany	32	34	36	38	40	42	44
Italy	36	38	40	42	44	46	48
Japan	5	7	9	11	13	15	17
North America	0	2	4	6	8	10	12
UK/Ireland	4	6	8	10	12	14	16
WOMEN – SHOES							
Europe	35	36	37	38	39	40	41
Japan	22	23	23.5	24	24.5	25.5	26
North America	5	6	6.5	7.5	8.5	9.5	10
UK/Ireland	2.5	3.5	4	5	6	7	7.5
MEN – SUITS AND COATS							
Europe	44	46	48	50	52	54	56
Japan	S	S	M	L	L	XL	XL
N. America/UK/Ire.	34	36	38	40	42	44	46
MEN – SHOES							
Europe	40	41	42	43	44	45	46
Japan	25.5	26	26.5	27.5	28	29	29.5
North America	7.5	8	8.5	9.5	10	11	11.5
UK/Ireland	7	7.5	8	9	9.5	10.5	11

These measurements may vary between different countries and manufacturers. They are provided as a guide only.

MEASUREMENTS

WEIGHT	
1 kilogram	2.2 pounds
1 pound	0.45 kilograms
1 kilogram	0.16 stone
1 stone	6.35 kilograms
VOLUME	
1 litre	0.26 gallons
1 gallon (US)	3.78 litres
1 gallon (US)	0.03 barrels

LENGTH/DISTANCE	
1 centimetre	0.39 inches
1 inch	2.54 centimetres
1 metre	39.37 inches
1 foot	30.48 centimetres
1 kilometre	0.62 miles
1 mile	1.6 kilometres
1 metre	1.09 yards
1 yard	91.44 centimetres

AREA	
1 sq metre	10.76 sq feet
1 sq foot	0.09 sq metres
1 sq metre	1.2 sq yards
1 sq yard	0.84 sq metres
1 hectare	2.47 acres
1 acre	0.4 hectares

TEMPERATURE

Celsius

Celsius = $5/9 \times$ (Fahrenheit −32)

–18   −10   0   10   20   30   37

0   10   20   32   40   50   60   70   80   90   100

Fahrenheit

Fahrenheit = $(9/5 \times$ Celsius) +32

TRAVEL PLANNING

DATE FROM/TO	DESTINATION

BIRTHDAYS & IMPORTANT DATES

DATE	EVENT

NOTES

paperblanks®
DAYPLANNERS

MIDI HORIZONTAL ISBN: 978-1-4397-3066-9
MIDI VERTICAL ISBN: 978-1-4397-3078-2
MIDI VERSO ISBN: 978-1-4397-3090-4

DESIGNED IN CANADA
PATENTED

North America 1-800-277-5887
Europe 800-3333-8005
Asia Pacific 800-3939-1771
Australia 1800-082-792

www.paperblanks.com

12 AR

paperblanks®
DAYPLANNERS

OCEAN SONG

Laurel Burch was a self-taught artist with an unmistakable style that was the manifestation of her love of life and fertile imagination. She created vibrant and moving themes with paint and paper, exquisitely embellished with gold and silver.

CHANT DES SIRÈNES

Douée de son tempérament intuitif, Laurel Burch poursuivit son travail artistique avec une vitalité créatrice étonnante. Témoignant de son amour pour la vie, elle a peint et dessiné des sujets joyeusement colorés, illuminés d'or et d'argent.

MEERESLIED

Laurel Burch war eine autodidaktische Künstlerin mit einem unverwechselbaren Stil, der ihre Liebe zum Leben ausdrückte. Mit Farbe und Papier schuf sie kraftvolle, ergreifende Werke mit erlesenen Verzierungen in Gold und Silber.

CANTO DI SIRENA

Lo stile inconfondibile di Laurel Burch, rivelò la sua natura fortemente immaginativa. Dalla sua fertile creatività nacquero soggetti vibranti, toccanti e variopinti, che l'artista trasferì su carta e lumeggiò d'oro e d'argento.

CANTO DO MAR

Laurel Burch foi uma artista autodidacta com um estilo inconfundível que foi a manifestação do seu amor à vida e imaginação fértil. Com papel e tinta, ela criou temas magníficos e animados, delicadamente ornamentados a ouro e prata.

CANCIÓN DE MAR

Laurel Burch fue una artista autodidacta cuya fértil imaginación le permitió crear con papel y pintura temas vibrantes y conmovedores, exquisitamente adornados con oro y plata, logrando un estilo inconfundible que reflejaba su naturaleza creativa.

paperblanks®

paperblanks®

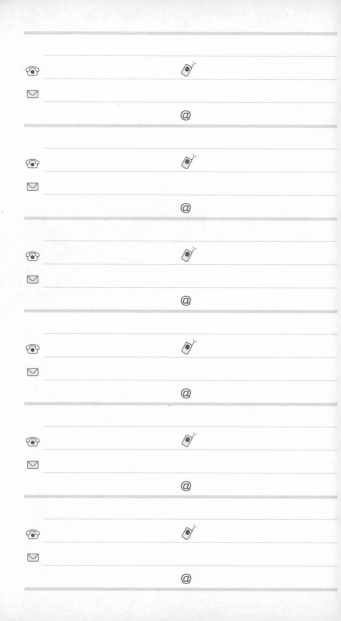

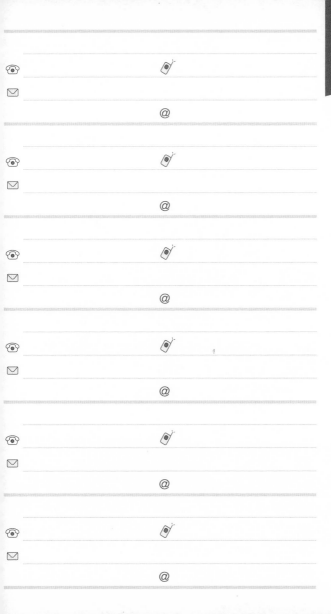

D
E
F

☎   📱

✉

@

☎   📱

✉

@

☎   📱

✉

@

☎   📱

✉

@

☎   📱

✉

@

☎   📱

✉

@

G
H
IJ

K
L
M

Z Pallette G
Crembrule 1x ✓ → eyeshad
Peach smoothi 1x ✓
Shimma Shimma 1x!
Goddess 1x ✓✗
Cupcake ✗ ✓